"God has kicked off an amazing year of women's ministry! My team and I are beginning Sue Edwards's Bible study this evening, and God has touched the hearts of sixty women to be part of it—we prayed for forty. Isn't He amazing? I couldn't be more excited about working where God is at work."

—Robin Neff
Fort Wayne, Indiana

"I have confidence when I dig into a study prepared by Sue Edwards that it will be solidly based on God's Word and will speak to me uniquely as a woman. Sue takes God's timeless truth and makes it relevant to me in ways that help me know my God better and love Him more as I live out my life with a feminine heart and mind. I always look forward to her next study!"

—Clarice Clayton
Arlington, Texas

"*Proverbs* helped us turn a corner in our Bible study program. The women found the study so practical and convicting that they began inviting their friends, and for the first time we had an energized environment. It was wonderful. This study of everyday wisdom from Proverbs drew the women back each week with an excitement we had not seen before. Life-changing convictions became the norm as we worked through the material together."

—Barbara Neumann
Director of Ministry to Women
Grace Community Bible Church
Richmond, Texas

"*Proverbs* was fabulous. It got us first into the biblical text, exploring subjects that were relevant and important. Then we had amazingly honest discussions about our lives and God's wisdom to make them work best! Thanks for being such a great resource for us. I so appreciate well-written material. It has been a blessing to use."

—Becky Byrne
Bible study leader
Clackamas Bible Church
Clackamas, Oregon

"We are so enjoying *Proverbs*. So timely for where we are today!"

—Brenda Croucher
Cypress Bible Church
Cypress, Texas

"I'm in need of more of the *Proverbs* study guides! Our group has grown and more of the women in our church have heard about it and would like to start another group. We've *really* enjoyed the study! I'm excited to see how God continues to use the study of Proverbs to challenge our women to wisdom living!"

—Beth Cunningham
Grace Community Church
Gresham, Oregon

PROVERBS

A SUE EDWARDS INDUCTIVE BIBLE STUDY

PROVERBS

Ancient Wisdom for a Postmodern World

Volume 1

LEADER'S GUIDE INCLUDED

SUE EDWARDS

Kregel
Publications

Proverbs: Ancient Wisdom for a Postmodern World, Volume 1

© 2007 by Sue Edwards

Published by Kregel Publications, a division of Kregel, Inc., P.O. Box 2607, Grand Rapids, MI 49501.

Library of Congress Cataloging-in-Publication Data
Edwards, Sue.
    Proverbs : ancient wisdom for a postmodern world / by Sue Edwards.
        p.   cm.
    Includes bibliographical references.
    1. Bible. O.T. Proverbs—Textbooks. 2. Bible. O.T. Proverbs—Study and teaching. 3. Christian women—Religious life. I. Title.
BS1467.E39 2007   223'.70071—dc22   2007017473
                                                          CIP

ISBN 978-0-8254-2547-9

Printed in the United States of America

07 08 09 10 11 / 5 4 3 2 1

To my grandsons,
Luke Edwards Boone,
Caleb Thomas Crook,
and
William Reed Boone.
May you emulate the wisdom of Proverbs
as you grow to be God's men.

Contents

Acknowledgments

Thanks to Jackie Roese and Barb Haesecke for their work on the "Probe the Passage" lessons, to Kelley Mathews and Tina Schieferstein for their editing expertise, and to Joye Baker for her friendship and support. I'm also grateful to Dennis Hillman, Steve Barclift, and Amy Stephansen (Kregel Publications) for their professionalism and integrity. And to my Dallas Theological Seminary colleagues and brothers in Christ: Mike Lawson, Lin McLaughlin, Mark Heinemann, and Jay Sedwick. You are Proverbs men, training up tomorrow's leaders, and I'm proud to serve beside you. And to my husband, David: I see Proverbs wisdom in you every day, and I thank God for the privilege of journeying with you.

How to Use This Study Guide

Women today need Bible study to keep balanced, focused, and Christ-centered in their busy worlds. The study questions in this guide allow you to choose the study level that fits your lifestyle. To provide even more flexibility, you may pick a different level each week, depending on your schedule.

- The "core" questions (designated by 1, 2, 3, etc.) require a total of about an hour-and-a-half of weekly study time, yet provide a basic understanding of the text. For busy women, this level offers in-depth Bible study with a minimum time commitment.

- The "Digging Deeper" questions require outside resources such as an atlas, Bible dictionary, and concordance. This level will challenge you to learn more about the history, culture, and geography related to the Bible. You will also be looking up parallel passages for additional insight.

- The "Summit" questions are for those who want to probe the text even more deeply. These questions grapple with complex theological issues and differing views. You're encouraged to investigate deeper by using an interlinear Greek-English text and *Vine's Expository Dictionary* on your own. Also you may create outlines, charts, and essays in seminary-style open-ended assignments. Some with teaching gifts and an interest in advanced academics will enjoy exploring the "summit."

Choose a realistic level of Bible study—one you can stick with. You may want to finish the "core" level first, and then tackle the other levels as time permits. Take time to savor the questions, and don't rush through the application. The key is consistency. Do not allow yourself to be intimidated by women who have more time or who are gifted differently from you.

Make your Bible study—whatever level you choose—top priority. Consider spacing your study throughout the week so that you can take time to ponder and meditate on what the Holy Spirit is teaching you. Do not make other appointments during the group Bible study. Ask God to enable you to attend faithfully. Come with an excitement to learn from others and a desire to share yourself and your journey. Give it your best, and God promises to join you on this adventure that can change your life.

What You Need to Know About Proverbs

How Proverbs Is Organized

A proverb is a short, pithy couplet that teaches truth in a memorable way. Here are two examples:

> An anxious heart weighs a man down,
> but a kind word cheers him up.
> —Proverbs 12:25

> If a man loudly blesses his neighbor early in the morning,
> it will be taken as a curse.
> —Proverbs 27:14

These short, pithy sayings begin in chapter 10 and end with chapter 29. Proverbs is structured like a sandwich with these brief, memorable sayings sandwiched between discourses at the beginning and at the end.

Here's another way to look at the organization:

Chapters 1–9	Incentives to seek wisdom from King Solomon
Chapters 10–29	Proverbs
Chapters 30–31	Insight on wisdom from Agur and King Lemuel's mother

A Note on Gender

In the two proverbs above, the nouns and pronouns are masculine. In English, we do not have a neutral gender, leaving the interpreters no choice but to translate either as masculine or feminine. The intent, however, is that these proverbs apply to all people, with "man" and "sons" used to represent the human race in general.

A Note on Bible Translations

The author used the *New International Version* (NIV) to write the questions in this study guide. We suggest you use this translation to study if you have one. Confusion can result when interpreters translate a single word of a proverb differently. Using the NIV will be helpful. If, though, you prefer to use a different translation, go ahead, but realize that occasionally you may sacrifice clarity.

Interpreting Proverbs Correctly!

Are Proverbs Principles or Promises?

Proverbs are principles that are true in general terms. They show us the way the world works and how to live wisely in it. If we live by wisdom principles, we will not bring calamity on our heads by our own foolish actions and attitudes. Foolishness is the source of many people's problems. When we are our own worst enemies, we bring problems upon ourselves either by being unaware of how the world works or by ignoring what we know.

The Proverbs Are Not Promises Made to Individuals

If we interpret proverbs as promises made to individuals, we're guilty of saying that God promises us something that He has not promised at all, and we confuse people regarding the Bible. It is crucial that we interpret the Bible in the way that the author intended.

A proverb is a pithy and wise saying. It's a few words pregnant with meaning. We must examine each word carefully and then dig for the overall meaning. When Benjamin Franklin coined the secular proverb, "A stitch in time saves nine," he was not promising that if you stitch up a hem before it unravels, it will never unravel again. He was explaining that if we attend to a situation early, we'll probably encounter fewer problems later. Franklin was using figurative language to paint a picture of the way the world works. Solomon was his predecessor.

When mothers read the proverb, "Train up a child in the way he should go: and when he is old, he will not depart from it" (Prov. 22:6 KJV), it's tempting to insist that God promises all prodigals will return. And God may give a mother that assurance. But God never makes that promise on the basis of this particular proverb. To insist that He has is to use bad interpretive principles. This proverb tells us that parents who do their best to understand their children and raise them in a godly home are more likely to see prodigals return to the faith than are those parents who never instructed them in the first place. But their turning to God is ultimately the child's choice. God does not override free choice for anyone. That's a principle He set in place from the foundation of the world.

Our task is to decipher the proverbs to learn timeless lessons about life, and then live in light of their truth.

Proverbs's purpose is to propel us into a relationship with God so we might live out the truths He shows us in this guidebook. They're valuable principles, but they are not promises. When we interpret proverbs as promises, we mishandle God's Word and mislead ourselves and others—and that gets us into trouble!

LESSON 1

Let's Build a Foundation

Discover the Author, Purpose, and Power

Are there timeless principles that govern life? Yes, they come from God the Creator, who alone knows how the world works. Has He revealed these principles to us? Yes, again. We find them tucked away in the Old Testament book of Proverbs—thirty-one chapters that promise to make us wise if we study them diligently and apply them wholeheartedly.

Do you want to make wise choices? Do you want to ward off danger for yourself and your loved ones? Do you want to be discerning, disciplined, and prudent? In short, do you want to be a woman who knows what to do in life's complex situations? If so, immerse yourself in the Lord's proverbs, and He will guide you through the maze of our postmodern world.

Discover the Author

1. Who wrote the book of Proverbs? What was his position? Who was his father (Prov. 1:1)?

2. Read 1 Kings 3:5–15. Soon after Solomon became king, God appeared to him in a dream, asking how He might help Solomon with his new responsibilities.
   a. Briefly, what was Solomon's petition (v. 9)?

   b. How do you think Solomon was feeling about his new role as king (v. 7)? What words does he use to describe himself? What was the attitude of his heart?

   c. What was the Lord's response? What do you learn about God from His response (3:10–13)?

d. What condition did the Lord place on Solomon in verse 14?

3. Read 1 Kings 4:29–34. Describe Solomon's wisdom and its impact upon his life.

4. What is the attitude of your heart as you begin this study? Are you willing to become like "a little child" in order to gain wisdom?

5. Why do you need wisdom? Are you feeling overwhelmed by some role or responsibility? Are you struggling with particular decisions or circumstances? How might a wise and discerning heart help?

6. Does it matter if you "walk in God's ways"? What is the relationship between obedience and wisdom? In what areas of your life do you need to listen to God in order to gain wisdom?

Solomon's brothers tried to steal his crown, and if they had been successful, he and his mother would certainly have been murdered. For the "cloak and dagger" account, read and summarize 1 Kings 1 and 2.

 Early in his reign, Solomon exhibited his wisdom when he acted as judge between two women. Read the account in 1 Kings 3:16–28. What happened? Why did this story make Solomon famous?

 Research Solomon's spiritual journey. How did his personal choices affect his relationship to God and his view of the world? What can you learn about his rule as king of Israel and his legacy (1 Kings 1–11; 2 Chron. 1–9; Ecclesiastes)?

Discover the Purpose

1. Read Proverbs 1:1–7.

2. In verses 2 and 3, Solomon explains that he wrote the book of Proverbs so we each might attain wisdom. Then he lists words that describe various aspects of wisdom. What are they? How are they different? Use a dictionary if necessary.

3. In verses 4–7, Solomon introduces us to the characters in Proverbs. Who are they? Are they different? Again, use a dictionary if necessary.

Discover the Power

1. Becoming wise will take more than self-disciplined human effort. In verse 7, Solomon reveals wisdom's power source.

   a. Write out this theme. (Note that "fear" is not terror but a reverent awe and respect for God.)

b. What do you think this verse means?

2. One of the most memorized proverbs is 3:5–6. What does it mean and how does it relate to discovering wisdom's power source?

3. The Bible speaks of two kinds of wisdom—human and spiritual. Read 1 Corinthians 2:6–16. What does this passage reveal concerning the difference? What is the source of spiritual wisdom? How is it different from human wisdom?

 For additional insight about human versus spiritual wisdom, read Paul's complete message to the Corinthians concerning wisdom (1 Cor. 1:17–2:16). What else do you learn?

So What? Personal Application

1. On what kind of wisdom do you rely upon the most? How is your life affected by your choice?

2. Read James 3:13–17.

a. Describe the life of a woman guided by spiritual wisdom.

b. List the primary evidences of a wise life.

c. As you examine the list describing spiritual wisdom, which quality do you struggle with least? Most? How might attaining spiritual wisdom affect your life this year?

LESSON 2

Why Seek Wisdom?

Why should we seek wisdom wholeheartedly? Solomon gives us many reasons by listing the benefits of a life devoted to wisdom. These are enticing incentives to take your Proverbs study seriously and make it a priority in your life!

You Will Stay Out of Trouble

1. Read Proverbs 1:8–19.

2. How does this apply to you? What do you think Solomon is trying to say in these figurative terms (vv. 8–9)?

3. Do you have friends who lure you away from what you know is good? What do they tempt you to do? How do they entice you? What is Solomon's advice (1:10)? What steps should you take to protect yourself?

4. Verses 11–19 give us a glimpse into the evil minds of criminals as they tempt the naïve to join them.
   a. Describe their invitation (vv. 11–12).

   b. What do they promise (vv. 13–14)? Why is it foolish to trust them?

   c. What ultimately happens to them and those who go with them? In what sense are they dumber than birds (vv. 15–19)?

d. How does someone end up in trouble—or worse, in jail or prison? What do you think draws so many people to violence and immorality? How can you protect yourself and loved ones from accepting this sometimes subtle invitation?

 People throughout biblical history have ignored wisdom principles and paid the price. Do a character study on one or all of the following women. What principles did each defy? What resulted? What are the lessons for us?
- Eve (Gen. 2–3)

- Rebekah (Gen. 27)

- Jezebel (1 Kings 16:29–21:24; 2 Kings 9:30–37)

You Will Stay Safe

Since God knows how the world works, He understands how you can put yourself in danger. You can protect yourself from consequences that put your life and loved ones at risk.
1. Read Proverbs 1:20–33.

2. In verses 20–33, wisdom is personified as a woman calling out to fools in the streets. If you approached her, what might be her demeanor? Summarize her questions found in verse 22. What is her heart's desire (v. 23)?

3. What consequences do fools face? Is there a time when it's too late to turn to Wisdom (vv. 24–32)?

4. What reward awaits those who listen to and heed Wisdom (v. 33)? In what ways does listening to Wisdom guarantee these rewards? In what ways does it not?

5. Why does God allow trials into our lives? What is wisdom's relationship to these trials?

 Do a character study on one or all of the following women. How did wisdom protect them? Glean principles for your life today.
   • Rahab (Josh. 2; 6:22–25)

   • Ruth (Ruth 1–4)

   • Esther (Esther 1–10)

   • The Widow of Zarephath (1 Kings 17:7–24)

You Will Live Longer

1. Read Proverbs 3:1–2.

2. Can you shorten or lengthen your life (3:1–2)? If so, in what sense? Can you give some examples?

3. In what sense are the number of your days set (Ps. 139:16)?

You Will Be Respected

According to Proverbs 3:3–4, can you generally enjoy a good reputation among your neighbors? If so, how? Is this a guarantee that everyone will like you (see 2 Cor. 2:15–16)?

 For a more in-depth study of believers abused for their faith, read 1 Peter 4:1–5. How do you think Christians should act toward fools and scoffers?

You Will Be Blessed

1. Read Proverbs 3:13–18.

2. How valuable is wisdom (vv. 14–15)?

3. How valuable is wisdom to you? What does your calendar and checkbook reveal? Do you desire anything more than wisdom? If so, what and why?

4. List the blessings promised in 3:16–18.

5. Do these verses guarantee you will have a large bank account, own several Mercedes, and live in a mansion? If you're wise, in what sense can you expect to be rich and blessed?

Prosperity theologians insist that every righteous believer is promised physical health and monetary wealth. They use verses like Proverbs 3:13–18 to substantiate their claims. Find verses to refute this false teaching. Examine the lives of Jesus, Paul, and others for insight. Write an argument refuting prosperity theology.

So What? Personal Application

How will your life be different if you seek wisdom with all your heart? Do you want to stay out of trouble? Do you want to live longer? Do you want to be safe and blessed and enjoy a good name among the community?

1. In this lesson, we've seen the rewards and benefits for those who attain wisdom. Are they worth your attention and effort? Examine your life honestly. What specifically hinders you? Rank the obstacles in order of difficulty. What do you need to do to gain wisdom this year?

2. Identify at least one obstacle that you want to overcome and ask God to enable you to overcome it this year. Pray, journal, or create something that expresses your heart's desire. Remember you must cooperate with the Lord as He works in you to accomplish change.

3. Envision yourself as a wise woman, loving God and life while having an impact upon others for good. That's what God and the leaders of this study want for you. Together, let's make it happen!

LESSON 3

Action Steps to Wisdom

Chapters 2–4 are packed with action verbs. Each chapter begins with a plea from God. He loves you dearly and has your best interest at heart. He knows that if you become wise, your life will be joyful and productive. But in order to gain wisdom you must cooperate with God by *doing something*. That's the way the world works. "If you do what you've always done, you will get what you've always gotten." So if you want to change, you must act differently. That's the only way to gain wisdom and enjoy all her benefits. This week we'll focus on Solomon's action verbs. Ask God to show you where you need to take action.

Priceless Treasures

1. Read Proverbs 2:1–15.

2. God, your Father, pleads with you in the first four verses. List the many action verbs in these verses.

    a. What do you observe about this list? What do you need to do first to attain wisdom? Then what?

    b. What are some practical, specific ways to live out these action verbs?

    c. What is the result if you do (2:5)?

3. Who is the source of our wisdom (2:6)? If He gives us wisdom, why do we need to take action? Explain how this works.

 Action isn't optional. Read James 1:22–25. What are you like if you focus on head knowledge but fail to apply what you learn? What is the promise?

4. Besides making people wise, how else does God use His wisdom (Prov. 3:19–20)?

 Study Wisdom's role at creation (Prov. 8:22–31). What was Wisdom's attitude as she partnered with God to create the world?

 Read *In the Beginning: Compelling Evidence for Creation and the Flood* by Walt Brown or other books on creation science.[1] What is the vapor canopy theory? The hydroplate theory? How do these theories explain the worldwide flood described in Genesis 6–8?

5. By acting on the action verbs you listed earlier, what other rewards can you expect (Prov. 2:7–8)?

6. What else will wisdom do for you (2:9–15)?

Honor and Discipline

1. Read Proverbs 3:1–12.

2. God, your Father, begins the third chapter with another plea (3:1). What is the plea? What is challenging about honoring this plea?

 Read Joshua 4:1–9. What did Israel do to remember how God worked in a special way in their lives? What can you do today to memorialize what God does in your life?

3. What are the verbs in Proverbs 3:5–6? What are ways to act on these verbs?

4. What's the warning given in verse 7? If that's your heart attitude, what's the benefit, found in verse 8? How do you think one affects the other?

5. What's the action verb in verse 9? What is your Father asking you to do, and why (3:10)?

6. Have you experienced verse 10? If so, describe what happened.

7. Does this passage promise that if you give to God, He is obliged to bless you with money? What principle is Solomon teaching?

8. Sometimes a father must discipline His daughter. What is a wise woman's response (3:11)? How do you think God's discipline appears in the lives of His daughters?

9. Why does God discipline us (3:12)?

10. Share a time when God disciplined you. How did you feel? What did you learn?

Sure Feet and Sweet Sleep

1. Read Proverbs 3:21–26.

2. What is the action verb in 3:21? What do you think this means?

3. Again, what are the benefits if you do (vv. 22–26)?

4. Why do you think Solomon keeps repeating himself in these introductory chapters before the actual proverbs begin in chapter 10? Why do you repeat yourself?

At My Father's Knee

1. Read Proverbs 4:1–9.

2. What does your Father ask of you next? List the action verbs in verse 1. How skilled are you at applying these instructions? What would those closest to you say?

3. In Proverbs 4:3–9, Solomon reminisces about his childhood. What picture does he paint of parent and child? Do you recall a time when your parents attempted to instruct you on an important matter? What was your attitude toward their instruction?

    a. If you were a compliant child, how did that benefit you growing up?

    b. If you were a rebellious child, how did that hurt you growing up?

    c. If your parents failed to instruct you, what effect did that have on your life?

    d. Who is available to instruct us all now?

4. Look closely at 4:4–9 and summarize David's teaching to his son Solomon. Again, list the action verbs. What did David encourage his son to pursue above all else?

5. If you are someone who has an influence on children, what are you encouraging them to pursue above all else?

The Road Less Traveled

1. Read Proverbs 4:10–27.

2. Where does your loving, heavenly Father promise to guide you (v. 11)? What do you think He means?

3. Describe your life if you stay on this path (vv. 12–13).

4. In 4:14–19 Solomon contrasts the two paths. How does he describe them? Why do you want to choose the straight path?

5. Which path does our culture tend to favor? List ways that our culture can sidetrack us. How can you protect yourself from the culture's negative influences and at the same time minister in it? If you've found ways to maintain your integrity while still shaping the culture, please share.

So What? Personal Application

1. To be a wise woman, you must guard your life carefully. You are of immeasurable value to God. Solomon lists four parts of your body that you must protect. What are they, and what do you think each part represents (4:23–27)?

2. Your life matters greatly to God. How much do you value your life? Are you careful to protect yourself from influences that will take you away from wisdom's path? If you are careless, try to identify why.

L E S S O N   4

Running Red Lights

In the first nine chapters, Solomon is preparing us for his pithy, practical couplets that begin in chapter 10. Over and over he exposes us to the benefits of wisdom as he pleads with us to get serious about life. But one subject is so hazardous, so alluring, he can't wait. He writes about it in chapters 2, 5, 6, and 7. What is it? A promiscuous lifestyle!

For women, the lure is often not so much the physical act, but the romance—that wonderful sensation of being wooed and adored by someone who can't eat or sleep for thinking of you. Whether you're married or single, the enemy can entrap you and take you down. Why are so many women vulnerable? What unmet needs are involved? And how can we protect ourselves?

Ask God to give you insight into this unspoken snare. Let's bring it out into the light and arm ourselves together.

Solomon assumes that the reader is married, as was customary in his culture for persons from the age of puberty. Although in our culture many marry later or remain single, the lessons still apply. Tailor them to fit your circumstances and remember to change the gender from masculine to feminine.

A Timeless Tragedy

1. Read Proverbs 2:16–22.

2. How can wisdom protect you (v. 16)? What was a common occurrence in Israel 3,000 years ago just as it is today (v. 17)?

3. What are the far-reaching effects of this practice?

4. Has this affected you or anyone in your family? Please do not use names and please share discreetly.

Read 2 Samuel 11 and 12—the story of Solomon's parents David and Bathsheba. How did their choices affect Solomon's life? Do you think his parents' actions may have shaped his convictions on this subject?

Read 1 Kings 11:1–3, 9–11. How was Solomon's life ultimately influenced by "strange women"? What's the lesson for us?

5. What is the ultimate consequence for those who choose this path and never repent (Prov. 2:18–19)?

A word to the divorced: Please do not dwell on the past. Divorce is never God's best, but there are reasons for divorce such as abuse, abandonment, and adultery. If you contributed to the divorce, ask God's forgiveness and ask Him to show you how to rebuild your life and protect yourself from making similar unfortunate choices in the future. Study this lesson carefully. God loves you and the future is bright as you seek wisdom with all your heart.

Run

1. Read Proverbs 5:1–23.

2. What is one of "Don Juan's" most powerful ways to tempt women (v. 3)? How can women today defend themselves from this tactic?

3. Where do these tactics lead (vv. 4–6)?

4. In the Old Testament Law, the penalty for adultery was stoning. This sentence was often reduced, however, allowing the offended party to take all the guilty party's worldly possessions as well as to make the offender his slave. Keeping this in mind, reread 5:7–10. What consequences await someone caught in adultery in our culture?

5. If you find yourself in tempting circumstances, what does the Bible tell you to do (Prov. 5:8; 1 Cor. 6:18; 2 Tim. 2:22)?

6. What are some ways women flirt with this temptation?

   a. How would you advise a married woman who's attracted to a friend's husband in a couple's friendship?

   b. How would you advise a single woman attracted to a married man at work?

   c. How would you advise a woman e-mailing a stranger on the Internet?

7. What will the offender say at the end of life (Prov. 5:11–14)? In your opinion, why is this the likely outcome?

8. Does God disapprove of sex? What does He suggest in verses 15–20 that shows He wants His children to enjoy sex in safe contexts?

Fool's Fire

1. Read Proverbs 6:20–35.

2. What does a prostitute make you (v. 26)? What do you think Solomon means?

3. What are the warnings in verses 27–29? What are ways we play with fire?

An Ancient Soap Opera

1. Read Proverbs 7:1–27. Let's reverse the gender and make the prostitute male—a gigolo.

2. What did Solomon see as he looked out his window? Describe the scene and the characters (vv. 6–10).

3. How did the gigolo act (vv. 11–13a)?

4. What did he say (vv. 14–20)? What might be some modern-day parallels?

5. Does his prey respond? How does Solomon describe the scene (vv. 21–23)?

6. What is Solomon's final warning (vv. 24–27)?

 Look up words like "adultery," "immorality," and "sexuality" in a concordance. What do other passages of the Bible contribute to our understanding of the subject of this lesson?

So What? Personal Application

1. Are you immune from these temptations (1 Cor. 10:12)?

2. We are all vulnerable. To help others, would you be willing to share a time when you were tempted? If so, please don't give names or details. What did you learn?

3. We can protect ourselves by "building fences." What are some of the fences you should be building? Do other women necessarily need to build the same fences? Discuss.

If you are struggling with romantic or sexual temptation in an unhealthy friendship or relationship, would you ask God to help you take needed steps to distance yourself from this situation and enable you to understand why you are drawn to this relationship? If you need confidential help, please inform your leader.

LESSON 5

The Power of Friendship and Community

"No man is an island," wrote John Donne. This is God's design. We were created for community, interaction, and companionship. It begins when we're born. Babies who are never touched will die, but those who are cuddled and nurtured will thrive. Marriages without communication shrivel and atrophy. People who physically or emotionally seclude themselves from others forfeit one of life's greatest joys—sharing themselves with others.

Yet many of us are lonely and fearful of connecting. We've been wounded by so-called friends or family, and have vowed to protect ourselves in the future. When we hide, though, we find that we cheat ourselves of one of life's richest blessings. Something inside each of us wants to be known and to know others intimately. God made us that way.

Although most of us would admit that we want friends, sometimes we don't know how to be a good friend. We don't know what to look for in a friend, nor how to set parameters to guard the friendship. Solomon's wisdom in Proverbs is a gold mine of truth, teaching us timeless principles on friendship.

If you seek deep, godly friendships and yearn to be a better friend, this lesson can help. Begin by asking God to reveal His personal truth for you and expect God to help you "show yourself friendly" (Prov. 18:24 KJV).

The Rewards of Good Friendships and Close Community

1. From Ecclesiastes 4:9–12, list the reasons it is great to have good friends and to be part of an authentic community. Why is it important to invest in intimate friendships?

2. From your list, give specific examples you have experienced.

Paul developed many friendships with coworkers. Study Romans 16 and describe Paul's relationships with some of his friends in Rome. What strikes you about this list of greetings? What do you learn about his friends?

Qualities of a Good Friend

A good friend is _____ (Prov. 17:17).

1. What kind of a friend is described in this passage? What sends some friends packing?

2. Have you ever had a friend like this? How did you feel? What did you learn?

 Jonathan and David were fast friends in the Old Testament. Their relationship reveals how to relate to one another today. Write their story in modern-day terms. What can you learn that will help you be a better friend (1 Sam. 18; 20; 23:16–18; 31:2; 2 Sam. 1:4–11)?

3. Why do some people want to be friends? What happens when that motivation vanishes (Prov. 19:4, 6–7)? What does this reveal about their hearts?

A good friend is _____ (Prov. 27:6; Eph. 4:15).

1. What do these passages tell us about real friends?

2. In contrast, what can flattery do to our friends (Prov. 29:5)? Can you think of any examples?

3. Have you ever had a friend who told you a hard truth? How did you receive it?

4. What was your friend risking? According to Solomon, why is telling the truth in love still acting like a real friend? What will usually happen (28:23)?

What happened when King David failed to be a true friend to his son Adonijah (1 Kings 1)? What are the lessons for us?

5. On the other hand, there are times when rebuking a friend is not wise (Prov. 17:9a). How do you know when to rebuke a friend or when to follow the advice of this proverb?

A good friend is _____ (Prov. 27:9, 17).

1. Read Proverbs 27:9. Can you give an example of a time when a friend's counsel was like perfume?

2. How can you develop your skills so you can help others in this way?

3. How can friends with different personalities and views help each other (27:17)? Have you ever enjoyed a friendship like this? If so, please describe it.

A good friend is not _____ (Prov. 25:17).

1. Solomon reveals ways we can sabotage a friendship. Have you ever had a friend who acted like the friend in 25:17? If so, how did you feel? How did it affect the relationship?

2. What is another way to irritate a friend (27:14)? What is the general principle?

3. Although your intentions might be the best, how might you unintentionally discourage a hurting friend (25:20)? What are some effective ways to minister to a friend's wounded heart?

4. What else can harm a friendship (26:18–19)?

5. Disagreements occur in the best of friendships. What can a friend do to end the quarrel (26:20)?

Throughout the New Testament, there are "one another" statements that help us develop close community. Use a concordance to locate these statements and list the lessons they teach (e.g., "encourage one another" is found in Heb. 3:13).

A Warning

The right friends are a blessing; the wrong friends can be a stumbling block!

1. How can our choices of friends affect our whole lives (Prov. 13:20)?

2. What is another danger (18:24)? Why could this be a problem?

3. What do you think Solomon means in 12:26? What are ways to follow his advice?

4. What kinds of bad companions are described in the following verses? How can you protect yourself?

a. Proverbs 1:10–15

b. Proverbs 17:19

c. Proverbs 18:1

d. Proverbs 22:24–25

The Perfect Friend

At times, friends are scarce. Who is the friend who is always with you? How is He the perfect friend (John 15:12–15)?

So What? Personal Application

Glance back over the lesson. Are you lonely? If so, can you discern why? Are friends a priority in your life? In light of the qualities discussed in the lesson, what kind of friend are you? Specifically, what can you do to be a better friend?

Get Organized!

Everyone wants a life that counts, but many of us don't maximize our potential. We fail to plan, organize, work smart, follow through, and pay the price required to develop our abilities and use our time effectively. Why? Our sin nature would make us sluggards. A sluggard is habitually lazy. A sluggard has excuses and rationalizes why her life is tedious, unfulfilled, and unproductive. We all fight laziness, and we can learn to better organize our lives as good stewards of the time God has given us.

> The wisdom of the prudent is to give thought to their ways,
>   but the folly of fools is deception.
> —Proverbs 14:8

> A simple [wo]man believes anything,
>   but a prudent [wo]man gives thought to [her] steps.
> —Proverbs 14:15

Solomon asks us, "Are you wasting your life for lack of discipline?" He wants to send us to his "School for Sluggards" so we can get more organized and enjoy the benefits of a diligent, blessed life.

Plan Ahead

Does God expect us to plan our lives? Yes and no.

1. What is the first step to an organized life (16:3)? Who is really in charge of our lives (16:4, 9)?

2. Nevertheless, what is our responsibility and what will generally result (21:5)?

3. Discuss the balance between planning for the future and giving God His rightful place as He directs our lives.

One of the great theological mysteries is the truth that God is sovereign over everything and yet our choices count. For insight into this mind-boggling reality, read *Evangelism and the Sovereignty of God* by J. I. Packer.[1]

4. Do you plan ahead? If so, share your strategy with the group. If not, what hinders you?

Portrait of a Sluggard's Sleep

1. What is the sluggard's relationship to her bed (26:14)?

2. What danger is there in loving too much sleep (19:15; 20:13)?

3. What is the motto of the sluggard (6:10)? What does Solomon ask the sluggard (6:9)?

4. What results from sleeping away the day (6:11)?

5. Do you love sleep? How much sleep do you need to be rested and ready to tackle the day? In your opinion, what is a healthy attitude toward sleep? How does too much sleep or lack of sleep affect your work?

 The Lord describes Israel's slumbering watchmen in Isaiah 56:9–12. What can you learn about the dangers of sleepiness and sloth from this passage?

Portrait of a Sluggard's Work Habits

1. Describe the picture of the sluggard in Proverbs 26:15. What is she doing? What do we learn about her work ethic? Can you recall a time when this happened to you?

2. What does the sluggard fail to do with her food (12:27)? What is the lesson for us?

3. What does the sluggard say to keep from having to go out to work (22:13; 26:13)?

4. Are you a procrastinator? List the excuses you make when you don't want to work.

5. What will ultimately result from a lazy, disorderly life (24:33–34)? Do you think any of these results are irreversible?

 Look up "work" in a concordance and study the related New Testament passages. What does God teach about the value of work?

6. Does a sluggard know about appropriate timing? What can you learn from Proverbs 20:4?

Portrait of a Sluggard's Mind-Set

1. What goes on in the heart and mind of the sluggard (13:4; 21:25–26)? What is the sluggard expecting from life? Have you ever felt the same way?

2. What do most sluggards think of themselves (26:16)? Why do you think they are deceiving themselves?

Portrait of an Irresponsible Sluggard

1. How does Solomon describe irresponsible people (10:26; 26:6)? What is he saying through this imagery?

2. How do you feel when you work with or rely on people who are lazy or fail to follow through? What kind of a witness is a lazy Christian?

Solomon's School for Sluggards: Learning to Overcome Laziness

1. Who is our role model in Solomon's "School for Sluggards" (6:6)? What does she teach us (6:7–8)? What else do you know about this tiny creature that might help us work smarter?

2. What is the warning in 12:11? Why is this such a hindrance to a productive life?

3. What else can hinder us (21:17)? Do you struggle with this temptation? How does it impact women today?

4. What is the lesson we learn from Proverbs 14:23?

5. Read Proverbs 14:4. This is a wonderful little proverb, rich in insight. Can you decipher its meaning? How can you apply it to your life today?

6. What lessons would you add to Solomon's curriculum? Have you learned any secrets to a productive life? If so, share with the group.

Rewards of the Disciplined Life

1. What is one blessing of the disciplined life (10:27)? Remember the Proverbs are principles (not promises), showing us the way the world generally works.

2. What is another benefit? Who also enjoys the fruit of your labors (14:26)?

3. Proverbs 22:29 describes the impact of a disciplined believer. See also 12:24. Describe her influence.

4. What is her impact on the world around her (14:34)?

5. Describe the journey of the organized, disciplined woman (15:19, 24). Are you serious about spending your days working hard for your God and His people? Is it worth the effort? If your life is a highway, where do you think God is leading you?

 Research Paul's work ethic. You may want to focus on his first missionary journey, which lasted about a year and a half, in which he covered over 700 miles by foot and over 500 miles by sea (Acts 13–14). What can you learn about discipline and diligence? Why do you think he was able to accomplish so much in such a short time?

So What? Personal Application

God dearly loves you, and your life counts. What have you learned that will make you a better steward of your days on earth?

LESSON 7

Word Power

In the first chapter of John's gospel, he referred to Jesus as "The Word." Through the person and teaching of Jesus we understand the heart and mind of God the Father. Unlike animals, we are endowed with the ability to form thoughts and to communicate them to one another and to God. This is a gift from God that enables us to know Him through prayer, both spoken and silent, as we utter the deep, innermost yearnings of our soul to a Father who listens and cares.

We know each other, and are known, by our words. They shape us; they distinguish us. When we open our mouths, we reveal who we are. Some of us are better with words than others. Some of us use words as weapons to manipulate and overpower others. Some of us use words to inspire and change the world for the better. Our ability to use words equips us for particular professions—lawyers, professors, authors, and preachers. Mothers soothe and sculpt their children by their words. Lovers use words to express heartfelt commitment and tender emotions. Generals use words that send soldiers into battle, ready to lay down their lives for their countries.

Words are powerful tools. We can choose to intentionally develop our word gift or to neglect it, to use it for good or for evil. At stake are our witness and our legacy. As you work through this lesson, pray that God will give you insight into the way you use words. In addition, ask Him to empower you to become a skilled wordsmith, using words that build others in their faith and bring Him glory.

Words "Я" Us

1. Jesus teaches us the origin of words in Matthew 12:34–35. Where do our words come from? What do they reveal about us?

2. Once uttered, are words simply forgotten (Matt. 12:36)? What is the basis for the judgment of nonbelievers? How do you feel as you read these verses? (Remember that the believers' judgment is the Bema seat of rewards.)

Write a theology of the Bema seat of rewards. (Biblical sources: 1 Cor. 3:1–15; 2 Cor. 5:1–10; Phil. 3:12–4:1. Books on the subject: *Your Eternal Reward* by Erwin Lutzer, *The BEMA* by Tim Stevenson, and *The Reign of the Servant Kings* by Joseph Dillow.)[1]

3. How much does God value good words? Do most people speak with care and understanding (Prov. 20:15)?

4. How powerful is the tongue? What do you think is the meaning of Proverbs 18:21?

The Power of Words for Good

1. Read Proverbs 15:30 and 16:24.

   a. Solomon used two images to show us the benefit of good words. What are these benefits and what do they look like in your mind's eye? Why do you think he chose these particular images?

   b. If you learn the art of choosing pleasant words, what good can you accomplish in people's lives?

2. When friends and loved ones are struggling with life, how can you help (12:25)? Can you recall a time when someone helped you through a trial? When you helped someone else? How did you feel?

 Paul was a master at encouraging his followers. Examples include Philippians 1:3–11; Ephesians 1:15–23; 3:14–21. Find other examples. How would you have felt if these words had been directed at you originally? What can you learn from Paul about encouraging others?

The Power of Destructive Words

1. According to Proverbs 12:18a, is it true that, "Sticks and stones can break my bones, but words can never hurt me"? Have you experienced a wound from words? Have you hurt others?

2. What happens when a person is barraged by a constant stream of wounding words (18:14)?

3. Proverbs 12:6 describes the power of words in an individual's life. Analyze this couplet. Throughout our lives, we all have received destructive as well as beneficial words from various sources. How do we overcome harmful words and the people who try to hurt us? Who has rescued you?

4. What is so tantalizing about a gossip's words? Are you tempted to gossip? Why do you think this is such a "pleasant" past time (18:8)?

5. What does Solomon call a slanderer (10:18)? Do you know the difference between gossip and slander? If so, inform your group.

6. What happens if we give in to the temptation to gossip and slander others (12:13)? Have you ever been "trapped" by something you said and later regretted?

7. How can we overcome the sin of gossip and slander? How can we discourage others who attempt to draw us into this sin?

When Words Fall Short

1. When are words not enough? What more is needed (14:23; 29:19)?

2. Some people are "charmers" with their words. What happens to the charmer in 26:23–26? Why do you think the author calls him a "coating of glaze over earthenware"? Have you been charmed by someone who was not what he or she seemed? If so, share the experience. (No names, please.)

3. Who is able to see through charmers (24:12)? How can you learn to see through them also?

Characteristics of Good Words

Good words are _____ (Prov. 12:17a; 16:13).

1. Solomon gives a courtroom illustration in 24:23–26. Whom does he applaud? How do their decisions impact nations? What happens to those who use words for dishonest gain?

2. What does God hate (12:22)? Name subtle ways our nation tolerates deceit.

3. In what ways are you tempted to dishonesty and deceit? Can you describe a specific time? Discuss.

Good words are _____ (Prov. 10:19).

1. What do these Proverbs reveal?
   a. Proverbs 10:19

   b. Proverbs 13:3

   c. Proverbs 17:28

   d. Proverbs 18:2

2. Are you a woman of many words? Has it caused trouble? If you have learned to curtail excess talking, share how you became an "undertalker."

Good words are _____ (Prov. 15:1; 25:15).

What kind of a person is pictured in 15:1 and 25:15? If you know someone who responds this way, describe him or her. Why is this person able to influence others and bring positive results?

Good words are _____ (Prov. 15:23).

1. Read Proverbs 10:32 and 15:23. Have you ever known anyone who was skilled with words like this? How did they minister to those around them? Can you recall an experience when someone ministered to you in this way? If so, please share.

2. What word pictures does Solomon use to describe these kinds of words in 10:20 and 25:11?

3. What rewards await those skilled with words (22:11)?

Jesus was the finest wordsmith the world has ever known. Study His interaction with those who were trying to trick Him in Luke 20. How did He use words to reveal what was in their hearts and to teach truth? Write out the principles you discover.

 PROVERBS

So What? Personal Application

1. Evaluate your words. It's easy to remember words that build and to forget our words that harm. Would others say you need to talk less or more?

2. Are your words timely and true?

3. Will Jesus praise you for your words at the Bema or will you be ashamed?

4. What do you specifically need to do to become a woman of wise words?

L E S S O N   8

Won't You Be My Neighbor?

High fences, long working hours, the Internet, fear—many factors keep people isolated, hidden away in their own little worlds. In our culture, our neighbors can live down the hall or across the street for years and we may never even know their names. In the Bible, our neighbors are not our Christian friends. Our neighbors are the people of the world, especially the people where we live, work, and do business. How should we treat our neighbors? Does it really matter to God if we are good neighbors? And why is "good neighboring" so important? Let's find out.

Who Is My Neighbor?

PROBE THE PASSAGE

Jesus lived in a world marked by social castes, prejudice, and religious hypocrisy. One day a religious expert, trying to save face and live for himself, challenged Jesus with this question: "Who is my neighbor?" In response, Jesus told the story of the Good Samaritan.

1. Read Luke 10:25–37 at least five days this week. On each day, before and after you read, ask the Holy Spirit to illuminate the passage for you.

2. During the week, meditate and ask yourself questions about Luke 10:25–37.

   - What is going on in the story?
   - Why did Jesus tell this story?
   - What is the main point of the story?
   - Was one idea particularly striking to me, that caused me to stop and think?
   - Why did God record this in the Bible for me?
   - How does this impact my life now and in the future?
   - What questions do I have about the passage?

   Don't be surprised if nothing jumps out at you right away. Don't be discouraged if you don't understand all you read. Be patient and probe the passage with questions.

3. Write your thoughts down.

Neighborly Ways

1. According to these proverbs, how are we to treat our neighbors?
   a. Proverbs 3:27–30

   b. Proverbs 14:21

 In Romans 13:8–14 and 15:2, Paul instructs us on our attitudes toward our neighbors. How do we "fulfill the law" toward neighbors? What principles can you uncover?

2. Some neighbors irritate us. They let their dogs bark at night, don't take care of their yards, or find other ways to infringe on our space.
   a. How does Solomon suggest we treat the irritating neighbor (Prov. 25:21–22)?

   b. What heart attitude does God ask us to display toward this neighbor (24:17)?

3. What is the warning to us in 25:17? Discuss healthy boundaries in relationships with neighbors.

4. What is the warning in 16:29? How can you genuinely care for your neighbor without putting yourself in danger?

5. Our culture is quick to take disputes to court. What is Solomon's advice in 25:7b–10? Why?

6. What should we do if neighbors—or even Christian friends—ask us to involve ourselves in financial deals, such as guaranteeing loans or investing money in their businesses? Read 17:18 and 6:1–5. What problems can result?

Neighborly Words

1. What kinds of words honor God and woo our neighbors to the Lord? What kinds of words drive them away?
   a. Proverbs 11:9

   b. Proverbs 11:12

   c. Proverbs 26:18–19

   d. Proverbs 29:5

2. Timing is important in any relationship. What is the advice in 27:14?

So What? Personal Application

Each year at our retreat I'm astounded by how many women say, "I came with my neighbor." Women most often come to faith through caring Christian neighbors in the midst of their communities. We are Christ's ambassadors, His witnesses to a hurting and sometimes hostile world. The term *Christian* means "little Christ," and that's our calling—to reflect Christ in our communities and our world.

1. Why is it challenging to be a good neighbor today? What is most difficult for you?

2. What do you think the Holy Spirit may want to teach you through this lesson?

3. What kind of a neighbor are you? What have you learned about "neighborliness" to help you reach out to those around you with genuine concern? Is there a specific application you can make right now?

Table Talk

(For Small-Group Discussion Use)

Directions for use: During discussion time, the discussion group leader will use this guide to lead her group through an analysis of Luke 10:25–37.

The Gospel of Luke: Early Christian writings identify the physician Luke as the author of this book and the book of Acts. Luke was a Gentile, who never met Jesus but heard about Him through the apostle Paul. Luke wrote this book sometime between A.D. 60 and A.D. 90. It was written to a Gentile named Theophilus to reassure him that God was still at work in the Christian community after Christ's ascension.

Luke 10 can be divided into three sections. Each section describes a different aspect of the Christian life. The first section, Luke 10:1–24, instructs us to be ambassadors, representing the Lord. The second section, Luke 10:25–37, instructs us to be neighbors, replicating the Lord. The third section, Luke 10:38–42, instructs us to be worshippers, responding to the Lord.

To hear what the Holy Spirit is saying to you through this passage, and to help you observe the facts, you must ask some questions: Who? What? Where? Why? How? No detail is too small. God loves for us to dig for treasures in His Word. This process of observing is very important and shouldn't be rushed. It is through this process that you discover and take away an understanding of what the author is saying. Many questions may come to mind as you read and reread. Ask them, write them down, and look up other Scripture passages to see what you can find. You may also want to read the passage in another version of the Bible.

What Does the Passage Say?

- *Who* are the people speaking in this passage (vv. 25–29, 36–37)?

- *What* questions did the man ask? List them in order.

- *How* does Jesus respond to the questioning?

- *Who* answered the man's questions?

- *How* would you describe the scene between the speakers?

- *Who* else might be present during this conversation?

- *Why* is the man asking the questions?

- *What* details can you observe about the people speaking?

- *Where* does the action in Jesus' story take place (vv. 30–35)?

- *Who* are the people in Jesus' story?

- *What* nationality are these people?

- *Who* are the Samaritans?

- *What* details can you observe about the people in the story?

- *What* is happening in the story? (Look for action words.)

- *How* would you describe the scene?

- *What* does the word *mercy* mean?

- *What* command did Jesus give the man in verse 37?

- *How* did this relate to the man's statement?

- *What* else did you observe in this passage?

Now that you have read and thought and questioned and gathered all sorts of facts and clues like an investigative reporter, it's time to move to the next step: interpretation.

What Does It Mean?

- *Why* do you think the man asked Jesus the questions?

- *What* do you think the connection is between the man's two questions (vv. 25b, 29)?

- *Why* do you think Jesus asked the man the questions in verses 26 and 36?

- *Why* do you think Jesus used the thief, priest, Levite, and Samaritan in His story?

- *What* is the main idea in Jesus' story?

- *What* do you think is the main idea in this passage?

These kinds of questions will help you better understand what the author intended. All of this is key in moving to the next question: "What is the Holy Spirit saying to me personally through this passage?" Here is where you go beyond seeing and understanding to recognizing that God, the Holy Spirit, is speaking to you directly through His Word so you'll know how to apply it to your life.

How Does This Apply to Me?

- *What* is the Holy Spirit saying to me in this passage?

- *What* is one way to apply this passage to my life (i.e., family, friendships, marriage, work, ministry, social life)?

LESSON 9

Blessed Are the Peacemakers

What should you do if a friend pulls you aside and says, "I'm so angry about the way Jane treated me yesterday"? Our tendency is to listen and empathize with our friends. We want to help them work through their anger and hurt. We've been taught that's what a good friend does. But if we're not on guard, we're drawn into sin. It's so easy to take up an offense for this friend and walk away angry with Jane, too. When that happens, the friend feels affirmed in her anger and is more likely to continue talking to others about Jane. This is how conflict is birthed and is spread to wound others and dishonor God. When our disagreements concern the family, the church, or the nation, the results are even more disastrous.

Conflict is like a country road: you never know where it's going to take you. God's Word contains clear instructions on how to resolve conflict, but these mandates are some of the most ignored in the Bible. Why? How does Jesus want us to respond to conflict? What would Solomon and New Testament authors suggest? This lesson tackles these hard questions with the assurance that if we apply what we learn, we will be blessed. Because Jesus promised, "Blessed are the peacemakers" (Matt. 5:9).

Jesus Says . . .

PROBE THE PASSAGE

1. In Matthew 18:15–17, Jesus gave us clear instructions about what to do when we face conflict. Read these verses at least five out of seven days this week. Ask the Holy Spirit on each day to illuminate the passage for you before and after you read.

2. During the week, meditate on the passage and ask yourself questions about Matthew 18:15–17.

   - What pattern or process do I see in these verses?
   - What is the main idea of the passage?
   - Was there an idea that was particularly striking to me that caused me to stop and think?
   - Why did God record this in the Bible for me?
   - What impact does this have on my life right now and in the future?
   - What questions do I have about this passage?
   - How might Proverbs 17:9 and 19:11 relate to this passage?

   Don't be discouraged if nothing jumps out at you immediately, or if you don't understand all you read. Be patient and keep probing the passage with questions.

3. Write your thoughts down.

Solomon Says . . .

1. How does God view people who constantly cause conflict (Prov. 6:16–19)?

2. According to Proverbs 17:19, how does God label people who enjoy conflict? Why are they so dangerous?

3. What should you do when someone tries to draw you into a conflict?
   a. Proverbs 17:4

   b. Proverbs 17:14

4. What will happen if you refuse to involve yourself in other people's conflicts (26:20)?

5. What will happen if you choose to involve yourself in other people's conflicts (26:17)?

6. Solomon paints word pictures of contentious women. What are they like? Do you see yourself in any of these descriptions?
   a. Proverbs 19:13b

b. Proverbs 21:9

c. Proverbs 21:19

d. Proverbs 27:15

7. If you're caught up in conflict, how will you probably feel (27:3)?

8. If you pursue peace, what benefits can you expect (3:17; 12:20; 14:30)?

Paul Says . . .

1. What should you do if you find yourself in the midst of conflict (Eph. 4:15)? What does this mean?

2. Why did Paul rebuke young widows in 1 Timothy 5:13? Why is it crucial not to act this way?

Study Romans 14 and extract principles that will help you extinguish a judgmental attitude and pursue peace.

 What happened in Philippians 4:2–3? What principles can you discover to help with conflict among women in the church?

 Paul's letter to the Ephesians is filled with counsel on ways to live as peacemakers with people who are different from us. What can you learn from 2:11–3:13?

James Says . . .

What can you expect if you are a peacemaker (James 3:18)? What does this mean?

Peter Says . . .

 Read 1 Peter 3:8–12 for Peter's instructions on how to be a peacemaker. What is the penalty if you cause conflict?

The Author of Hebrews Says . . .

 What are the instructions in Hebrews 12:14–15? What can happen if we do not follow God's design concerning conflict?

So What? Personal Application

Are you faithful in following the Bible's instruction concerning conflict? Be honest. Spend some time prayerfully asking God to reveal your actions and attitudes. If you struggle to obey, attempt to discern why. What do you need to do to become a peacemaker? If you've learned to live by these principles, share with your group the blessings you've enjoyed as a result.

Table Talk

(For Small-Group Discussion Use)

Let's apply what we've learned to real-life situations. Read the case studies and then discuss the questions to help you prepare to be a peacemaker.

Case Study #1

Dear Jesus,

I've been going to church for three years. Shortly after I began attending, I joined the worship team. One of the vocalists was a woman named Jan. She's an outspoken woman who serves in other areas of ministry in our church.

Jan missed our practices regularly but would appear on Sundays, expecting to sing for Sunday service. At times the worship leader would make music changes during practice. Jan would learn of those changes during the sound check on Sunday morning. She'd become irritated and oppose the changes, claiming they were changed "without telling her." Then she'd do things her way during the service, at times throwing the rest of the vocalists off-key.

Overall I avoided Jan as much as I could. One night during choir she overhead me talking about a job opening at my office. She applied and got it!

The first few months went well. Jan learned quickly and had a good attitude about her job. Then one day, Jan made known the conflict she was having with the pastor of our church. I knew she had issues with our pastor, but didn't know (and didn't want to know) the details. Unfortunately, she voiced them anyway.

As time went on in the workplace, she continued to publicize her conflict with our pastor. At times she'd listen to my phone calls and, if I were talking to someone from the church, she would make comments about my conversation. She also kept in touch with other families who'd recently left the church and complained to them.

I felt pulled in two directions. Our pastor had always helped me in my spiritual walk. So the very people Jan was talking about were the ones I turned to when I needed assistance, guidance, or a listening ear. I was trying not to be swayed by Jan's comments. Jan told me things about these people that I didn't want to know and didn't believe were true. But eventually there was just a shadow of a doubt in my mind.

Finally, I went to the associate pastor, and he gave me some ways to work through this problem with Jan. Meanwhile, I continued to pray that the conflict would be resolved. I asked God to soften Jan's heart, take away her resentment, and guide her in a more faithful walk.

About a month later, Jan announced she and her family had left our church and started attending another. Jan really liked this new church. Occasionally, she'd feel the urge to bring up past issues, but I changed the subject by talking about her new church. Now that her church life is settled, her work environment seems to need "improvement." She's starting to voice her displeasure with our workplace.

Jesus, what would You have me do?

Signed,

Carol—Coworker in Distress

Discussion Group Questions

- Why do you think people in the church allowed Jan to behave like she did?

- Why do you think Carol allowed Jan to behave like she did?

- Do you allow the "Jans" in your life to behave like this? If so, why?

- According to your lesson this week, what did Carol do that was biblically correct?

- What did Carol do that was incorrect?

- Where should Carol seek wise counsel?

- Drawing from your lesson, what are some different ways Carol could have dealt with this situation?

- What are the possible outcomes of this situation?

- What are some biblical principles you can personally apply in your life from this case study?

Case Study #2

Dear Jesus,

My friend Emma has struggled for years to love and honor her mother-in-law. All the while her mother-in-law has continued to be critical and manipulative. Emma has tried to talk to her husband about this situation but he isn't responsive. At one point she went to her mother-in-law to discuss her feelings but it wasn't received well, and nothing changed. She has sincerely prayed for a change of attitude, for love towards her mother-in-law, and for a forgiving heart.

Emma and I have been friends for a long time. On occasion, she'll share with me what's going on between her mother-in-law and her. I know we're supposed to seek wise counsel and be vulnerable and honest, but here's my question: Where is the line between friends sharing one another's burdens, and listening to complaining and gossiping?

What would You have me do?

Signed,

Wendy—Want to Do It Right!

Discussion Group Questions

- How would you apply Matthew 18:15–17 to this situation?

- From your lesson, what other Scripture references apply here?

- Wendy refers to Galatians 6:2, "Carry each other's burdens, and in this way you will fulfill the law of Christ," and Proverbs 15:22, "Plans fail for lack of counsel, but with many advisors they succeed." If you were to give counsel to Wendy, how would you balance these verses in light of Matthew 18:15–17?

- What other factors influence your decision on how to handle this case study (e.g., the heart of the person, the character of the person, the intent of the person, the outcome of the conversation, etc.)?

- Has this situation ever happened to you? Considering what you have learned, how could you have handled the situation differently, better, or more biblically?

- What is the one principle the Holy Spirit wants you to implement personally?

Case Study #3

Dear Jesus,

Recently I went back to my hometown for a wedding. While there, I ran into an old high school friend named Sally. She had grown up in a Christian home, had a solid reputation, and had married a man from a prominent family in the community. She had two children and had divorced her husband because she believed he had been sexually abusing their children. Sally shared how her ex-husband's family pulled strings and kept the case from going to court but that she was able to get a settlement in which her husband could no longer have contact with the kids.

A few weeks later, I was in my back yard talking to Claire. She was recently divorced and had moved in next door with her six-year-old son, Andrew. During our talk, she told me that a man had moved in with her, and through our conversation I learned it is Sally's ex-husband!

Now what do I do? Should I tell Claire what my friend Sally said? Or is that gossip since the courts didn't convict him of any crime? If I remain silent, am I putting Andrew in jeopardy?

I decided to talk to Claire about what I'd heard. She didn't want to hear it!

A few weeks later another neighbor, Olivia, mentioned that her little boy was happy to have a new friend on the block. He'd met Andrew recently and played at his house often.

As she told me of the boys' friendship, my thoughts were racing. *Claire's boyfriend doesn't work so he's home with the boys during the day, which means Olivia's son will be in the house with this man. What if he harms this little boy and I never said anything? Could I live with myself? Am I overreacting?* I decided to share with Olivia the "hearsay" I'd heard from Sally.

After I shared this information with Olivia, I called Claire and told her about my conversation with Olivia.

Claire is extremely angry with me and accused me of gossiping.

Jesus, what would You have me do?

Signed,
Julie—Just Not Sure

Discussion Group Questions

- Drawing from your lesson, what did Julie do correctly?

- What did she do incorrectly?

- Some conflicts aren't so clear-cut. What makes this case study difficult to fit into the Matthew 18 formula?

• Drawing from the lesson, Matthew 18, and other Scripture passages, come up with some different ways Julie could have dealt with this situation.

• Where should Julie go for wise counsel?

• What should Julie do now (with Claire, Olivia, Sally, the man, etc.)?

• What are the possible outcomes of this conflict?

• What would Jesus say to Julie?

• From this case study, what can you apply to your own life right now?

Training Guide for Small-Group Leaders

Studying God's Word together is an exciting adventure, requiring a leader. Thank you for your willingness to lead the group. Your role as leader is to guide a discussion characterized by

- a nonthreatening climate conducive to an honest exchange of ideas;

- a flow of stimulating and meaningful interaction;

- the presentation of God-honoring, biblically based insight.

What can you do to help the group succeed?

1. Put the Women at Ease

Express care for the women from the moment the first woman walks in the door until the last woman leaves. Greet them as they arrive. Initiate conversation before the discussion begins. Draw out women by asking nonthreatening questions such as "How long have you lived here?" or "Tell me a little about yourself." Especially focus on the woman who seems shy or lonely. Provide name tags to help women learn each other's names. Set an atmosphere of unconditional love and inclusion where women can relax, learn, and share.

- *Be other-centered!* This is not the time to visit with your best friend. You are your group's shepherdess! Many women are in dreary circumstances and have varied spiritual needs. Make walking into your group a highlight of their week!

- *Develop good listening skills.* By intentional, focused listening, you convey that the participation of each group member is valued.

You may be the only reflection of Christ some women ever see!

2. Begin and End on Time

Get started on time even if only two or three are there. Late arrivals will soon learn they must be prompt. There will always be stragglers. Begin without them. Quickly and graciously greet them when they arrive. And honor women's busy lives by ending when you said you would, but allow women who want more fellowship to remain behind and enjoy visiting.

3. Begin with Enthusiasm

Ask someone who is enthusiastic to answer the first question. Get off to an exciting start! Keep your eyes off your study guide as much as possible. Look at the women as they are speaking. Train yourself not to read lesson notes or the introductory paragraph word for word but instead rephrase it and speak it out in your own words.

4. Assume Authority (but Remain Gracious)

- Be firm but not bossy.

- Be gentle but stay in control.

Someone has to be in charge, and you are it! The women expect you to lead. Project your voice if you are soft-spoken. Sit up and direct the group. You are there to keep the group on target and make sure time is not wasted. This is a serious role but don't forget to maintain your sense of humor and have fun.

5. Encourage Discussion: DO NOT LECTURE!

The discussion group leader is *not* a lecturer. After the discussion, you may want to wrap up the study with a formal lecture, but during the discussion the leader does not teach. She does not spotlight herself as the one with the answers but instead focuses on the women in the group. Her role is

- to direct the flow of the discussion;

- to encourage interaction;

- to set the climate or tone;

- to guard against poor use of time;

- to lead the group in an understanding of the material.

Establish an atmosphere of unconditional acceptance where each member is free to share what she's thinking and feeling. We may not always agree with a woman's view, but we can respect her by listening thoughtfully to her ideas.

As a leader you do not correct or "straighten out" women in the group. Avoid saying "No," or "But . . ." Some possible responses when you hear an unusual answer are,

- "I've never thought of it in that way."

- "That's an interesting perspective."

- "I see what you are saying."

We want an atmosphere where each woman shares what the Holy Spirit is teaching her through God's Word. Women need to feel they can ask their questions and not be made to feel foolish.

It's also imperative, though, that a biblical perspective be presented. Draw out women with solid biblical insight to present their views when the group needs to hear a biblical answer. In this way, women hear the biblical perspective, but no one in the group is singled out as the one with the wrong answer. As women continue studying the Bible, they soon discover God's perspectives for themselves.

6. Consider Calling on the Women by Name

This is better than asking for a volunteer to answer the question because

- usually the same few women volunteer;

- waiting for volunteers consumes time, causing the discussion to drag.

This is also your greatest tool for maintaining control! You can bring out shy women while keeping talkers from dominating. Call on the quiet women early in the discussion because often when they have participated and been affirmed, they find it easier to speak up. If you prefer not to call on women by name, do your best to give everyone an opportunity to participate.

Move quickly through questions with obvious answers. For example, observation questions can be answered easily right from the text. Call on one person and then move on, or quickly answer the question yourself as a transition to other kinds of questions.

Spend most of the discussion time on sharing and opinion questions. Sharing and opinion questions bring out interesting discussion. Your ultimate goal is to encourage natural interaction. As the women become more comfortable, you'll see a more natural interchange, with women speaking up in response to one another. This makes the group less like a question-and-answer schoolroom session. That's good!

This type of discussion, however, takes more skill to control. If the group becomes chaotic and the quieter ones are not participating, step back in and take control. Otherwise, let this more natural interaction continue—but learn to sum up ideas expressed and move on to the next question when appropriate. You are responsible for the flow of discussion.

7. Use Volunteers for Share Questions

Let the women know that personal application questions are for *volunteers only!* It's inappropriate to ask a woman to reveal personal information unless she's ready. Our goal, however, is to share our heartaches and struggles. How can you facilitate a deep level of personal sharing? *Be ready to share on personal application questions occasionally.* Be real with the group! A great benefit of discussion groups is that we build community when participants open up about their fears or feelings of inadequacy. Guard against spending too much time, though, working through personal problems. Life's answers are found in Scripture.

8. Be Sure Every Comment Is Affirmed!

The leader must be sure every comment is acknowledged in a positive way. Nothing feels more awkward than to express an idea and have it ignored. This conveys rejection. If no one else in the group interacts or responds to the comment, then the leader must affirm the group member with warm words like, "Thank you for your insight," or at least, "That's an interesting way of looking at it." Try to respond as you would in everyday conversation, as naturally as possible. *Affirming the women is a necessity!*

Quick affirmations besides "good point":

Excellent	Fantastic
Super	Great answer
Wonderful	Terrific

Wow	Fabulous
Absolutely	I agree
What insight	That was deep
I like that	Wish I'd thought of that

Some affirmations for the group are

- "I'm so happy to see all of you!"

- "There are many places you could be today, and I'm so glad you chose to be here!"

- "Thank you for being so well prepared"

- "I appreciate each one of you and the effort you made to be here."

9. Keep Up the Pace

The pace of the discussion is determined by the personalities of the group members and the skill and preparation of the leader. Observe the pace of your group. Is it peppy or does it drag? Develop strategies to keep the group moving and interesting. There are two extremes, and each requires a different response.

A. *The quiet group.* Does your group hesitate to answer? Do you feel like you are "pulling teeth" to get them to participate? Then you have a quiet group. They often water-ski over issues and are content with pat answers. Their pace is too slow—it drags—and they tend to finish quickly. But when the discussion is over, it wasn't very interesting. What can you do to perk up a quiet group and shoot it full of energy?

- Muster enthusiasm.

- Encourage, encourage, encourage.

- Be patient; intimacy takes time.

- Ask energetic women to interject stimulating questions to spark interest.

- Draw out answers by calling on many women for each question.

- Don't settle for a pat answer.

B. *The talkative group.* This group has difficulty finishing the questions because so many women want to participate. The pace is perky and fun, but the discussion is easily sidetracked. When you go down rabbit trails, you talk about issues unrelated to the Bible study. This is frustrating for women who want to understand and apply the passage. When you seldom finish the lesson, the more serious students become discouraged.

The group is filled with women who love to talk and have interesting ideas to contribute. The problem comes when the more verbal women dominate those who are less articulate and when the group can't get through the lesson. What can you do?

- Assume a greater air of authority.

- Privately elicit the more talkative women's help in drawing out quieter women.

- Cut off talkers (as graciously as possible).

To refocus a group, here are some things you could say:

- "In the interest of our time remaining, let's move on."

- "Let's pick up the pace a little."

- "Let's finish that discussion after Bible study."

- "Let's finish our questions, and then we'll come back to this."

Whenever the group is sidetracked, the leader must decide how much time she will spend there. Pursue a rabbit trail *briefly* if it is of common interest and time allows. Then get back to the meat of the lesson. Do your utmost to finish every week. The women expect it!

What should you do if a woman breaks down in tears? This *special circumstance* can stall the pace and tempt the group to get sidetracked for the rest of the lesson. *DON'T!*

Be sensitive but also think of the group as a whole. The group often wants to spend the remaining time consoling, counseling, and fixing the problem. You can't! Allow a couple minutes of tender feedback, but then step in and *pray briefly* for the woman. Assure her you will talk with her later. Then move on. Later, talk with her privately and give her your encouragement and support. But *do not discontinue working through the lesson.*

10. Control Your Own Talking

The leader is in ministry to others. This is the participants' time! If the group is talkative, the leader should limit her talking. If the group tends to be quiet, talk to prime the pump and then back off when the women are participating.

11. Maintain Unity of Spirit

Never speak in a critical manner about any church or denomination, and do your best to discourage this kind of talking in the group. Redirect the conversation. This kind of criticism is divisive, destroying the unity we're striving to build. A woman in the group may be offended if another group member slanders a group she grew up in or respects. Avoid politics.

12. Stay in Touch with Your Group

Keep in touch regularly with your group—by phone or e-mail. If you never contact them, you're sending them a message that you don't care! Let them know that you're praying for them—especially if they're absent. This builds relationships. If a new member joins the group, be sure to call the first week to answer any questions and familiarize her with group procedures. You are a shepherdess—so tenderly nurture your flock.

Will Your Group Pray Together?

If so, here are suggested methods:

- Let the women know that there will be prayer time and ask them to submit a *personal* request.

- Encourage the women to write out their requests as they do their lesson rather than waiting to do so after they arrive.

- Ask your group to write down their prayer requests on 3 x 5 index cards.

- Collect the cards and *you* (the leader) read the requests aloud to the group. Share any answered prayer at this time.

- Either pass the cards back out to the group or place them in the middle.

- Ask the group members each to pick a card and pray for the request during the group prayer time or during the week.

- As the leader is reading the requests, the women can write them down, or one person can keep a group prayer journal.

- A volunteer can e-mail the requests to group members.

Leader's Guide

BEFORE YOU BEGIN . . .

I'm delighted that you've chosen *Proverbs: Ancient Wisdom for a Postmodern World* to enrich your understanding of God's Word and help others in the process. Familiarize yourself with this overview as you prepare to lead the study and invite women to join you.

Purpose of the Study

Life is confusing. One expert says, "Watch out for fats—they'll clog your arteries and kill you!" Another insists, "No, stay away from carbs—they're the real enemy." Next year, another so-called breakthrough will contradict yesterday's findings. We often hear contradictory voices telling us how to live. Where can we discover timeless truths? In God's Word—specifically the book of Proverbs. Solomon wrote Proverbs to show us how the world works and how to become wise women.

Organization of the Study

"What You Need to Know About Proverbs" (pages 12–13) shows how the study is organized and how to interpret Proverbs. This information will help you explain the study to interested women and teach it correctly.

Key Words: Wisdom and Fear

Help participants understand these important words. *Wisdom* means "skill in living." Wise women know how to make prudent decisions in their everyday lives. The Hebrew word for wisdom is *hokmah*, referring to the skill of craftsmen, sailors, singers, and administrators—knowledgeable, experienced experts in their field.

Psalm 107:27, for example, describes sailors in a violent storm: "They reeled and staggered like drunken men; they were at their wits' end." The original language reveals that their seafaring skills were useless. The author refers to these skills as *hokmah*—wisdom, the ability to *do* something.

Exodus 28:3 provides another example. The author writes, "Tell all the skilled men to whom I have given wisdom in such matters . . . to make garments for Aaron, for his consecration, so he may serve me as priest." Moses commands the Israelite tailors and seamstresses to make an exquisite garment for the priest. The passage says these skilled tailors possess the spirit of wisdom. They not only knew about tailoring; they were skilled at *doing* it!

Women face important decisions daily. Do they want to know what to do in complex circumstances? If so, this study is for them. The book of Proverbs was written to make women wise—to show them the best way to handle whatever comes their way.

Wisdom begins, though, with a right relationship to God, bringing us to our second key word—*fear*. The theme verse of the book is Proverbs 9:10: "The fear of the LORD is the beginning of wisdom, and knowledge of the Holy One is understanding." Some women are confused about the meaning of the word *fear*, especially if they grew up hearing more about God's wrath than His love. They think of fear as terror. That interpretation, however, is wrong. Fear of the Lord refers to reverence and awe, not dread or anxiety. As you encounter this term throughout the book, remind women of its proper meaning.

Four Groups of Proverbs People

As you navigate your way through Proverbs, you'll encounter four different kinds of people. Distinguish between them. These groupings help you understand people and their varying responses to God's instructions, an important skill required to be wise.

- Simpletons (The Simple): ignorant people who need to be taught
- Fools: impulsive, unbalanced people who resist God's instruction and hate discipline
- Mockers: wicked scoffers, evil people who ridicule God's wisdom and attempt to snare others
- Wise people: upright, humble, and righteous people who seek God's instruction

Resources

Allender, Dan B., and Tremper Longman III. *Bold Love.* Colorado Springs: Navpress, 1993, 229–309. A good book for an in-depth study on the people of Proverbs.

To listen to an introductory lecture by the author, go to http://www.irvingbible.org/index .php?id=133 and select *Proverbs*, then "Introduction: Germinate Wisdom." Browse the site for other lectures to complement Proverbs lessons.

LESSON 1: LET'S BUILD A FOUNDATION

Get Acquainted

Open with prayer. Should you pray or invite one of the participants to do so? Be sensitive to the women. If they're comfortable praying out loud, give them opportunity. If not, you, as the leader, pray. Then spend time getting to know one another. You might, for example, ask each woman to introduce herself by telling something about family, hobbies, what she likes to do on a Saturday night, a pet peeve, or what she hopes to gain from the study. If time allows, spend your first meeting connecting with questions or icebreaker games. For an extended community builder, ask participants to name the wisest person they've ever known and explain why.

Get Focused

Look over the study guide with your group and express your excitement about the topic. Discuss ground rules. If women join later, remember to orient them. Stress the importance of confidentiality.

Some women come to Bible study for the sole purpose of studying Scripture. Others come for community, to find friends. Regardless of your own bent, honor both desires. We all need a relationship with God through serious Bible study *and* we all need relationships through connecting in authentic community. Be sure the schedule provides time for both.

Discuss Lesson 1

To enhance your small-group leading skills, study the "Training Guide for Small-Group Leaders" on pages 74–79. Leading a small group is a complex task, requiring lots of practice. Be patient and reread the Training Guide often.

Did you ask women to come prepared to discuss the first lesson? If so, begin by quickly summarizing the introductory page to focus their minds on the day's topic. Guide the group through the study by reading the questions and drawing the women into discussion and discovery. Your role as leader is *not* to illumine the group with your answers but to provide a safe place for them to share what God is teaching them. Set an atmosphere where they can respectfully explore different ideas. Roadblocks to spiritual maturity become dismantled in these kinds of groups.

Don't expect deep sharing for the first few weeks. Women on occasion do bond quickly but often they need time to trust one another. If you find that time prohibits the group's discussing all the questions, plan ahead. Choose blocks of questions to cover and eliminate others, or skim over observation questions and spend time on opinion and application questions.

Lesson Content

Lesson 1 chronicles the life of Solomon, beginning with his request for wisdom as a young king and culminating with his downfall as a result of his disobedience later. Also students will be introduced to four kinds of Proverbs people and the concept of the fear of the Lord, both explained on page 81. To ensure application, include "So What? Personal Application" questions in your discussion (page 17).

Resource

To hear a lecture on this subject by the author, go to http://www.irvingbible.org/index.php?id=133 and select *Proverbs*, then "Wed the Head, Hands, and Heart If You Want to Be Smart."

LESSON 2: WHY SEEK WISDOM?

Troubleshooting

Lesson 2 enumerates the benefits of seeking wisdom. Solomon insists that wise women are more likely to stay out of trouble, enjoy safety and security, live longer, and be blessed and respected. During the discussion, participants sometimes ask, "Then why do bad things happen to wise women?" If you encounter this question, remind them that proverbs are not promises but general statements about the way the world works. Those who seek wisdom generally will enjoy these benefits, but bad things still happen to good people.

Women who, for example, eat in healthy ways, exercise regularly, and see their doctors periodically generally live longer. This is the way the world works. Some individuals, though, are struck down in their youth by accident or disease. Nevertheless, the principles are true. But life is mysterious, and so are the ways of the Lord.

Also, believers enjoy long life when they live wisely—yet children die. Again, this is not a promise of a particular number of years on the earth, but a statement that those who seek wisdom will not cut short their years by foolish actions that lead to premature calamity.

In addition, children who are loved unconditionally, disciplined fairly, and trained carefully will usually grow up to love the Lord. Other factors, however, come into play, such as free will and bad companions. Life is complex. If your group struggles with these issues, reiterate the concepts presented in "What You Need to Know About Proverbs: Interpreting Proverbs Correctly!" (pages 12–13).

Do any of the group's participants adhere to prosperity theology? This view insists that every righteous believer is promised physical health and monetary wealth. Prosperity theologians use Proverbs to substantiate their claims, often confusing believers. If women in your group hold this view, gently remind them that Jesus, Paul, and other biblical characters did not enjoy physical health or monetary wealth—nor does the Bible promise this for all Christians. Suggest women consider John 16:33; 2 Timothy 3:10–12; and James 1:2–3 as they wrestle with this issue. Remind them to listen respectfully to everyone's ideas, even when they disagree.

Creative Arts Ideas

The "So What? Personal Application" questions (page 23) focus on hindrances to wisdom. How can you help women express ways to overcome these hindrances? Consider these creative activities.

- Ask each woman to write her obstacle on biodegradable paper, then dig a hole outside, and bury it. We planted small flowers over the buried papers to symbolize the growth and beauty we expected as we immersed ourselves in God's Word throughout the coming year. As the women watched the plants grow and blossom, they were reminded of their own "growth" in wisdom as a result of their study. If weather does not permit this exercise, consider purchasing artificial plants. Place the papers on the bottom of the pots and use the plants as centerpieces.

- Ask participants to write their obstacle on a piece of paper. Line a container with foil. Then burn the obstacles, symbolically showing God's power to overcome these roadblocks in their lives. If you're meeting in a church, check with your building supervisor for guidelines in using fire, and, of course, be careful.

- Nail the papers to a cross or other object. Display the object throughout the study to remind the participants that God can enable them to overcome whatever threatens their spiritual growth.

LESSON 3: ACTION STEPS TO WISDOM

Will You End with a Wrap-Up Message?

Leading small groups and teaching are different skills. The "Training Guide for Small-Group Leaders" (pages 74–79) provides sound principles to help you lead your group. Note that when you wear your small-group leader's hat, you do not lecture! But you may want to end your time by putting on a teacher's hat. Participants often enjoy hearing a message to crystallize biblical truth.

Your wrap-up might be a ten minute informal presentation, allowing for interaction and questions, or a forty-five minute formal lecture, more like a pastor's message on Sunday. If your study consists of several small groups, you may prefer a formal lecture. If you're meeting in a home, your group may prefer a more interactive format. Use what works for you and your group.

Resources to sharpen your teaching skills are listed at the end of lesson guides. Feel free to draw from the teaching messages at http://www.irvingbible.org/index.php?id=133, citing your sources, of course. These messages are available to either individuals or to groups. If you believe, though, that God may want *you* to teach the Bible, step out and try.

Women love to hear their own leaders teach them rather than hear virtual teachers on DVD or over the Internet. At first, your skills may not be as honed as more experienced teachers, but in time you should improve. And you have advantages over a virtual teacher. Women need models they can watch, hug, and talk to. And when one of their own steps out and is used by God, it inspires everyone to step forward and use their gifts, too. So if something in you says "teach!"—then go for it!

Enlist Women to Teach with You

Other women have something to say that would benefit the group. Listen attentively when they tell how God works in their lives. Identify women who inspire others. Who holds a high view of the Bible and has spent time studying? Who walks close to Jesus? Who lives wisely? Who is articulate? Passionate? Growing? Mature?

Beginning with lesson 5, the study will focus on particular kinds of wisdom. Future lesson topics include, for example, authentic community, organization and discipline, neighbors, and peacemaking. Some students may be experts on these topics, modeling wisdom and integrity and having life experience to share. If so, consider asking these women to prepare a testimony or message for the entire group that week.

Presenters also need a cooperative attitude. When you give a woman the platform you give her influence. I've worked with a few women who took advantage of this opportunity. They spoke twice as long as time allotted. Or they refused to prepare, wandering aimlessly. Or they became so emotional that they broke down, upsetting women in the study.

To alleviate these problems, set a time limit and ask women to write out what they will say. Insist they review their message with you. Stress that if they're a "time hog," group time will be shorter, irritating group participants. Use wisdom as you select women presenters, but consider how much women will benefit by hearing a variety of voices.

Creative Arts Idea

Suggest participants attend in gym attire—the way they might dress to walk, run, or work out. Their outfits will remind everyone that the focus of the lesson is action. To be wise, we must take action! Stress that dressing this way is, however, voluntary, especially if some women go to work or other functions after the study.

Resources

Mathews, Alice P. *Preaching That Speaks to Women*. Grand Rapids: Baker, 2003.
Robinson, Haddon. *Biblical Preaching: The Development and Delivery of Expository Messages*. 2d ed. Grand Rapids: Baker, 2001. (See also http://www.Christiancourses.com for an online course.)

Stott, John. *Between Two Worlds: The Art of Preaching in the Twentieth Century.* Grand Rapids: Eerdmans, 1982.

Willhite, Keith, and Scott Gibson, eds. *The Big Idea of Biblical Preaching: Connecting the Bible to People.* Grand Rapids: Baker, 1998.

LESSON 4: RUNNING RED LIGHTS

Lesson Content

In my experience, lesson 4 creates more discussion than any other lesson in the study. The subject—women's struggles with romantic and sexual temptation—is taboo in many churches. Yet women struggle with sexual desires and attractions just as men do. The motivation and needs are often different, but the temptations are just as real. As a result, participants welcome the opportunity to bring these issues into the light and learn wise responses.

Please be sensitive to single and divorced women during the discussion. The introduction contains a note to singles and "a word to the divorced" (page 32). While we should never encourage or condone divorce, neither should we ostracize divorced women. Create an ethos in which women in various situations are free to share what they've learned, even from poor choices.

Help your group see that hiding is harmful. Think of an oozing wound on your arm. Instead of inspecting it carefully, treating it with antibiotic, and exposing it to the air to heal, you simply slap a Band-Aid on it and go your way. My husband tells the story of his great grandmother's unnecessary death. When she was shelling green beans, a piece lodged deep in her finger nail bed. Busy and distracted, she ignored the injury. Soon, infection festered, but she continued to disregard red streaks and swelling. Ultimately toxicity spread, killing her. Ignoring or hiding sin kills too.

Hiding ultimately makes us vulnerable to *more—not less—sin*, especially sexual sin. It has become the sin above all sins—horrible, appalling, beastly, heinous, shameful—and unspeakable, the one sin that we hide at all costs, the one sin we don't share with our spouse or best friend. It is *the* taboo subject. Few teach or preach about it. Leaders rarely admit they struggle—and what stays in the dark has a secret place to grow, the perfect incubator.

When we hear about couples who leave the church to divorce without ever asking for help, we wonder why. Yet we know how easy it is to hide behind a mask of spirituality. Will church people accept, understand, and aid us when we confess our sin to one another? We are embarrassed, afraid, and proud. Often, our willingness to confess depends on the sin.

Sins on the "approved list" are easy to confess—selfishness, pride, anger, even general lust . . . but it's dangerous to confess sins on the black list. Specific sexual sins rank high there: habitually savoring a forbidden sexual fantasy in your mind, deliberately pursuing a risky relationship with a married member of your small group or work, surfing the Internet for pornography in the middle of the night. Listen to the words of a pastor who hid his sexual addiction for ten years, all the while carrying on his day-to-day responsibilities in his church and speaking all over the country.

> I wish we in the church did a better job, conveying God's love for sinners. From the church, I felt mainly judgment. I cannot bring my sin to the church until it has been neatly resolved into a warm, uplifting testimony. For example, if I had come to the church in

the midst of my addiction to lust, I would have been harshly judged. That, in fact, is why I had to write my article anonymously. Even after the complete cycle of confession and forgiveness, people still wrote in comments, "The author cannot possibly be considered a Christian." . . . We in the church could learn from Alcoholics Anonymous. Somehow they require accountability and communicate the Immanuelness of God. He is with you when you succeed and when you fail. He does not wait with folded arms for you to pick yourself up out of the gutter. His hands are stretched out toward you, eager to help. Where are the hands of the church?[1]

Jesus' hands are eager to embrace sinners who are bound in sexual sin. He doesn't condone their sinful acts or attitudes. He doesn't wash away the consequences of their sin. He demands that they change. But He does so in a way that is respectful and not demeaning. His magnetic love compelled them, calling them into the light. We are called to do the same.

This lesson may surface women who need help. Are you willing to meet privately? Suggest resources—books, conferences, and counselors.

Resources

Dillow, Joseph C. *Solomon on Sex*. New York: Nelson, 1977.

Dillow, Linda, and Lorraine Pintus. *Intimate Issues: 21 Questions Women Ask About Sex*. Colorado Springs, CO: Water Brook Press, 1999. (See http://www.intimateissues.com to learn more about their conferences.)

Edwards, Sue, Kelley Mathews, and Henry Rogers. *Mixed Ministry: Working as Brothers and Sisters in an Oversexed Society*. Forthcoming, 2008.

LESSON 5: THE POWER OF FRIENDSHIP AND COMMUNITY

A New Focus

Lesson 5 is the first topical lesson drawn from Proverbs chapters 10 through 30. Beginning with chapter 10, proverbs are recorded randomly, on a variety of subjects. I've grouped the proverbs on specific subjects of particular interest to women—lesson 5 on friendship and community. Women will be looking up and studying proverbs from throughout chapters 10 through 30 on this particular topic. This approach helps us dig deep into one aspect of wisdom.

Remember that a proverb is a short, pithy couplet that teaches truth in a memorable way. Instruct participants to ponder each proverb for its deep, rich meaning. When we study biblical accounts, we study the whole account and then attempt to discern biblical principles. When we study Paul's letters, we read portions of the letter and then try to understand the meaning for us. Studying proverbs is different. We won't cover large sections of Scripture. Instead, we slow down to ponder each couplet carefully, as if we were mining for diamonds, deeply buried and tiny but beautiful and many faceted.

Resources to Help Interpret Proverbs

If you need help interpreting Proverbs, consider these fine books:

Bridges, Charles. *Proverbs: An Introduction and Commentary.* The Tyndale Old Testament Commentary Series. Carol Stream, IL: Tyndale, 1964. Reprint, Downers Grove, IL: InterVarsity, 1981.

Waltke, Bruce K. *The Book of Proverbs: Chapters 1–15.* New International Commentary on the Old Testament. Grand Rapids: Eerdmans, 2004.

———. *The Book of Proverbs: Chapters 15–30.* New International Commentary on the Old Testament. Grand Rapids: Eerdmans, 2005.

A Note on Bible Translations

Remind the women that the author used the *New International Version* (NIV) to prepare the study guide. Don't require them to use this translation, but suggest they do if they own one. Confusion can result if an interpreter translates a single word of a proverb differently.

Troubleshooting

Lesson 5 asks women to label qualities of a good friend and then answer questions related to each quality. Participants should fill in the blanks, reflecting the answers below:

- A good friend is *loyal and steadfast* (Prov. 17:17).

- A good friend is *honest, truthful, and genuine* (Prov. 27:6; Eph. 4:15).

- A good friend is *wise, challenging, and gives good counsel* (Prov. 27:9, 17).

- A good friend is *not overbearing, smothering, or jealous* (Prov. 25:17).

Expect different perspectives as women fill in this final blank, and discuss the suggested proverbs. Help them see that a good friend employs healthy boundaries, is not intrusive, understands the importance of good timing, and does not use humor to hurt others.

Question 3 (bottom of page 39) should help the women minister effectively to hurting friends. Draw out skilled women, experienced in working with the wounded and discouraged. When a friend is downhearted and discouraged, a ministry of presence is more helpful than, for example, "singing songs" and quoting inappropriate Bible verses.

Creative Arts Ideas

- Ask women to come prepared to discuss these questions: "Who has been a good friend to you? Why?" They might bring a picture or an artifact that helps the group understand the relationship.

- Show a painting that expresses friendship or community. Ask the women what they see and what genuine Christian community and friendship means to them.

- Listen to a contemporary song about friendship. Display the words and discuss its meaning.

Resources

Cloud, Henry, and John Townsend. *Boundaries: When to Say Yes, When to Say No to Take Control of Your Life*. Grand Rapids: Zondervan, 1992.

Gorman, Julie. *Community That Is Christian*. 2d ed. Grand Rapids: Baker, 2002.

LESSON 6: GET ORGANIZED!

Lesson Content

Does God want us to plan ahead? Do we direct our lives or does God? Women in our studies often struggle to understand the balance between planning for the future and giving God His rightful, sovereign place. The first question set, "Plan Ahead," guides women to think through and discuss this tension. Draw out women who understand that a wise woman plans carefully and lives a disciplined life, but remains flexible, entrusting everything to God.

Work your way through each question set. Don't water-ski over the passages. Don't settle for incomplete or haphazard answers. Challenge the group to discover together the beauty of these proverbs. Keep up a brisk pace so you will have time to tackle the wrap-up application question ("So What? Personal Application," page 47). This lesson challenges women to recognize excuses to be lazy, to remember their days are numbered, and to invest themselves wisely in kingdom work. Our culture promotes indulgence, but the Bible exalts self-discipline and hard work.

Troubleshooting

The second question set, "Portrait of a Sluggard's Sleep," asks women to study proverbs that paint pictures of lazy people. For example, Proverbs 26:14 says, "As a door turns on its hinges, so a sluggard turns on his bed." Picture a woman who is tied to her bed, rolling back and forth, over and over, but unable to get up. Solomon shows us what happens when we sleep too much—we become lethargic and unproductive. Help participants understand the importance of healthy lifestyles.

The third question set, "Portrait of a Sluggard's Work Habits," continues to paint pictures of lazy people—they exhibit such a poor work ethic that they're too lazy to feed themselves, or to cook their food. Of course, these are extremes for effect. In the section "Portrait of an Irresponsible Sluggard," Solomon compares irresponsible people to vinegar to the teeth and smoke to the eyes (Prov. 10:26). In this imagery, he highlights that lazy people are irritating and exasperating.

Participants are often confused by Proverbs 14:4, "Where there are no oxen, the manger is empty, but from the strength of an ox comes an abundant harvest" (question set, "Solomon's School for Sluggards," question 5 on page 46). This pregnant proverb explains that life is messy. In our work, marriages, and child-rearing, we encounter problems that complicate our lives. But ultimately, through these entanglements come rich blessings and learning experiences.

Resource

Mackenzie, Alec. *The Time Trap: The Classic Book on Time Management*. 3d ed. New York: American Management Assoc., 1997.

LESSON 7: WORD POWER

Lesson 7 meddles in the topic of women's conversations, sometimes raising guilt and regret. Pray that God will use this lesson to convict women of that sin. Work hard to create a positive atmosphere where women can confess, be forgiven, and determine to change. As the leader, be a fellow struggler. We talk so much it's impossible not to misuse words. Nevertheless, our goal is to become women who use words to build up and tell the truth in love. What kind of group atmosphere fosters this kind of spiritual growth?

Create a Positive Group Ethos

Ethos (*e-thas*) is a place's distinguishing environment or atmosphere. As the leader, you set the ethos, and although you cannot see it, women respond positively or shut down in response. Every home has ethos. In some homes children experience unconditional love and fair discipline. As a result they usually grow up confident and secure. Other homes exude a chill—children walk on eggshells, knowing that performance earns affection, easily withdrawn when they mess up.

Ethos has an impact in classrooms. In some classrooms, students feel comfortable to ask questions, even dumb ones. They know the teacher has their best interest at heart and won't intentionally embarrass them. In others, students don't dare open their mouths. Why? Ethos.

And your small group has ethos, highly influencing participants. Will it be a place where women can voice their deep hurts and difficult questions? Can they sense God's love? Can they be honest and do business with God there? Forgiveness and healing take root in places like that. To learn how to create positive group ethos, review the "Training Guide for Small-Group Leaders," focusing on the importance of affirmation and controlling your own talking. Remember, group time is not about you! It's about giving women a safe place to discuss what *they* learned, try out *their* new ideas, and articulate *their* convictions.

Troubleshooting

The question set "Characteristics of Good Words" includes blanks for women to fill in, reflecting the spirit of the answers below:

- Good words are *true and honest* (Prov. 12:17a; 16:13).

- Good words are *few* (Prov. 10:19).

- Good words are *gentle and patient* (Prov. 15:1; 25:15).

- Good words are *appropriate and timely* (Prov. 15:23).

Lesson 7 is long. Move through at a brisk pace to ensure you cover the last question set, "So What? Personal Application." These questions challenge women to take inventory and action—the ultimate purpose of our study! If you lead a talkative group, making it difficult to finish the lesson, consider these strategies:

- As the leader, summarize observation questions, and then ask the group the opinion and sharing questions.

- Eliminate question sets altogether and focus on the sets that you believe will be of greatest benefit to your particular group.

- Divide the lesson into two parts and cover the questions in two separate sessions.

Gossip and Slander

Question 5 on page 50, question set, "The Power of Destructive Words," asks, "Do you know the difference between gossip and slander?" Help the group understand that gossip is sharing a confidence that is true but inappropriate or unkind. Slander is spreading lies. Both are sin, damaging unity in the community and destroying relationships. To gossip or slander is like tearing open a feather pillow on top of a windy mountain. It is as difficult to reclaim the damaging words as it is to collect the feathers.

LESSON 8: WON'T YOU BE MY NEIGHBOR?

A New Format

Lesson 8 is a "Probe the Passage" format supplemented with questions similar to those in the previous lessons. The lesson begins by asking women to read Luke 10:25–37, "The Parable of the Good Samaritan," at least five times during the week, and then answer recommended questions. The purpose of this exercise is to teach women to study the Bible for themselves.

As you prepare to lead your group through lesson 8, find "Table Talk" at the end of the lesson (pages 59–60). You may want to limit your discussion to this section. Read the instructions carefully. Three main questions are provided, followed by multiple examples. (What does the passage say? What does it mean? How does this apply to me?) Careful Bible scholars, preachers, and teachers use three steps in their approach to studying the Bible—observation, interpretation, and application—a method reflected in the "Probe the Passage" format. These methods ensure proper and thorough handling of the text. To learn more about this method, see *Living by the Book* by Howard Hendricks and William Hendricks.[2]

Initially, we didn't know whether the women would find this format overwhelming or helpful. We were pleasantly surprised. We prepared women for the change. We encouraged them by telling them that we believed they could, and would, rise to the challenge. They did, and feedback indicated they enjoyed the process.

Options

Several options are open as you lead the group. Pray and determine which option best fits the needs of your group.

- Guide the group through the "Table Talk" questions and then supplement with a short wrap-up.

- If you're not ending group time with a teaching wrap-up, ask some of the supplemental questions, especially the "So What? Personal Application" questions.

- Cover all the supplemental questions in addition to "Table Talk."

- Break the lesson down into two separate sessions to allow for a more thorough treatment of the subject. Include creative arts ideas and/or action steps.

Creative Arts Ideas

- Create an on-the-spot drama, asking women to play the people in the parable. Seeing the scenes cements them in women's minds. Discuss what you learned after actually walking through the story.

- Secure a DVD of the Gospel of Luke and play the scene where Jesus tells the story of the Good Samaritan.

Action Steps

- Brainstorm ways your group might tackle a community project together. Consider working in the community once a month or for a season, living out what you are studying.

- Play a DVD that explains a community ministry, or invite someone from the ministry to visit and enumerate ministry opportunities.

- Ask each woman to come prepared the next week to share her testimony.

Resources

McDowell, Josh, and Don Stewart. *Answers to Tough Questions Skeptics Ask About the Christian Faith.* San Bernardino, CA: Here's Life Publishers, 1980.

Newman, Randy. *Questioning Evangelism: Engaging People's Hearts the Way Jesus Did.* Grand Rapids: Kregel, 2004.

LESSON 9: BLESSED ARE THE PEACEMAKERS

Another "Probe the Passage" Format

Review lesson 8's "A New Format" and "Options" (pages 90–91) if you need a refresher on how to use the "Probe the Passage" format. Lesson 9 contains three sections, listed below. Determine which section or combination of sections will best equip your group to become skilled peacemakers.

- Jesus' instructions in Matthew 18:15–17

- Additional advice from Solomon, Paul, James, Peter, and the author of Hebrews

- Three case studies (see "Table Talk")

Matthew 18:15—17—Basic Peacemaker Training

This familiar but often neglected passage contains three steps. If the group fails to discover the process you may want to put on your teacher's hat and summarize the process *after* the discussion.

Step 1: Go and Show

There are two parties in the conflict: the offender and the offended. Both are assumed to be Christians. Jesus instructs the offended to be the initiator. Also, the offense is termed a sin. Consider these questions before you respond: Is the offense truly a sin, or could it lead to sin? Are you evaluating an action you've observed or a heart attitude you suspect? Can you overlook the offense (Prov. 19:11)? Can you interact with the offender without this offense coloring the relationship? If not, you need to discuss the conflict openly, *just between the two of you.* Jesus limits the first meeting to the two parties—and no one else should know about the conflict.

Step 2: Take Witnesses

If the first meeting is unfruitful, the offended party is responsible to call a second meeting and invite witnesses—those who may have insight concerning the offense—or a neutral party to help sort out relevant details. Be sure the witnesses are acceptable to both parties. Witnesses often serve as catalysts to bring about truth and a joyful resolution.

Step 3: Take It to the Church

If there is still no resolution, Jesus says, "Tell it to the church." Whomever God has placed in authority over you in the church is now in charge. Courtesy dictates that all parties are heard at the same time, and godly people follow the directives of their leaders.

Case Studies

Applying biblical principles to real-life situations is complex and challenging. Discussion group questions follow each case study to help the group decipher appropriate responses. Expect, and respect, diverse opinions. The objective is not to come to a consensus but to wrestle with options. When we actually experience conflict, we know more of the details and can depend on the Holy Spirit's guidance. Our insight in a case study, though, is limited. Help group members apply biblical principles while giving them freedom to discuss possibilities. The exercise should embolden them to face conflict, even in messy situations; apply sound biblical principles; and become peacemakers in their daily lives.

Ask a group member to read the case study, and allow plenty of time to discuss the questions that follow. If the discussion heats up, step in and remind women to listen respectfully and disagree agreeably. Explain the limited nature of case studies and their purpose.

Resources

Sande, Ken. *The Peacemaker: A Biblical Guide to Resolving Personal Conflict.* 3d ed. Grand Rapids: Baker, 2004.

Shelley, Marshall. *Well-Intentioned Dragons: Ministering to Problem People in the Church.* Minneapolis: Bethany House Publishers, 1994. (For ministry leaders.)

For additional resources, training, and professional mediators, please check out Peacemaker Ministries at http://www.HisPeace.org.

Notes

Lesson 3: Action Steps to Wisdom

1. Walt Brown, *In the Beginning: Compelling Evidence for Creation and the Flood* (Phoenix, AZ: Center for Scientific Creation, 1995).

Lesson 6: Get Organized!

1. J. I. Packer, *Evangelism and the Sovereignty of God* (Downers Grove, IL: InterVarsity, 1961).

Lesson 7: Word Power

1. Erwin Lutzer, *Your Eternal Reward* (Chicago: Moody, 1998); Tim Stevenson, *The BEMA: A Story About the Judgment Seat of Christ* (Gainesville, TX: Fair Havens Publications, 2000); and Joseph Dillow, *The Reign of the Servant Kings: A Study of Eternal Security and The Final Significance of Man* (Hayesville, NC: Schoettle Publishing, 1992).

Leader's Guide

1. "The War Within: Part 1," *Leadership Journal* 3.4 (Fall 1982): 4. This article can be found online at http://www.LeadershipJournal.net/special/sexclassics.html.
2. Howard G. Hendricks and William D. Hendricks, *Living by the Book* (Chicago: Moody, 1991).

About the Author

Sue Edwards is assistant professor of Christian education (her specialization is women's studies) at Dallas Theological Seminary where she has the opportunity to equip men and women for future ministry. She brings over thirty years of experience into the classroom as a Bible teacher, curriculum writer, and overseer of several megachurch women's ministries. As pastor to women at Irving Bible Church and director of women's ministry at Prestonwood Baptist Church in Dallas, she has worked with women from all walks of life, ages, and stages. Her passion is to see modern and postmodern women connect, learn from one another, and bond around God's Word. Her Bible studies have ushered thousands of women all over the country and overseas into deeper Scripture study and community experiences.

Sue is the author of *New Doors in Ministry to Women: A Fresh Model for Transforming Your Church, Campus, or Mission Field*, and *Women's Retreats: A Creative Planning Guide*. Kelley Mathews coauthored both books and is currently partnering with Sue and Henry Rogers on a book about men and women working as brothers and sisters in our oversexed society (scheduled to be released in 2008).

Sue has a doctor of ministry degree from Gordon-Conwell Theological Seminary in Boston and a master's in Bible from Dallas Theological Seminary. With Dr. Joye Baker, she will be overseeing a new Dallas Theological Seminary doctor of ministry degree in Christian education with a women-in-ministry emphasis, beginning summer 2008.

Sue has been married to David for thirty-five years. They have two married daughters, Heather and Rachel, and four grandchildren, Becca, Luke, Caleb, and Will. David is a CAD applications engineer, a lay prison chaplain, and founder of their church's prison ministry.

More Studies to Help You Grow

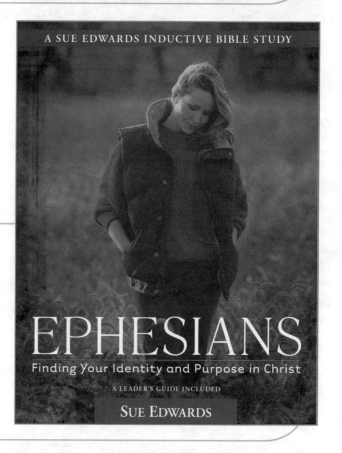

Discover the Wisdom of God

This insightful companion to Sue Edwards's inductive study of Proverbs explores more selections of ancient wisdom. In this nine-week study, Sue guides readers as they explore these timeless life lessons and apply them to our postmodern world.

978-0-8254-2548-6 • 96 pages • $11.99
Coming in October 2007!

Living a Victorious Christian Life

The church in Ephesus was surrounded by debauchery and occultism, yet Ephesian believers persevered as strong Christians. Using Paul's advice to this fledgling church, Sue shows readers how to stay strong in Christ in any situation through this nine-week Bible study.

978-0-8254-2549-3 • 96 pages • $11.99
Coming in October 2007!